AGAINST NATURE:

WILDERNESS POEMS

Judith McCombs

American Dust Series # 9

© Judith McCombs   1979

$2.95/paper, $7.95/cloth, ISBN 0-913218-84-7/pa,
0-913218-83-9/cl

Dustbooks
P.O. Box 1056
Paradise, CA 95969

Library of Congress Cataloging in Publication Data

McCombs, Judith.
    Against nature.

    (The American dust series ; no. 9)
    I. Title.
PS3563.A26219A7   811'.5'4   77-28749
ISBN 0-913218-83-9
ISBN 0-913218-84-7 pbk.

Table of Contents

ACKNOWLEDGMENTS

Many of these poems have appeared in *ambit,* the blewointment press, *end of the world speshul, what isint tantrik speshul,* the Coach House Press, *This Is My Best, Connections, The Fault,* the Glass Bell Press, *Broadsides, Green River Review, Jeopardy, Loon, Michigan Hot Apples, Modern Poetry Studies, Moving Out, Poetry Northwest, Prison International, Red Cedar Review, Wascana Review, Waves, Wayne Literary Review,* and *Works.* "The Habit of Fire" and "In Praise of the Natural Flowing" appeared first in *Poetry,* cxxvii, No. 4 (January 1976), 205-7.

Others of these poems are scheduled to appear in *Images, Northern Light,* and the Rhiannon Press *Anthology.*

Image

In the summer photo
a diagonal of orange
traverses the wilderness
thickets & ridges
we failed to inhabit

Against Nature

Here by the lake & its useless ripples
I'm noticing things, I can't help it
There are relics of insects again in the food
There's a wilderness behind me, I know, I paid
to get out here & it's chock-full of dirt

In a place without gates how can you open
Without windows what do you see

My habits won't work, out here, & yours
won't either (see, the fishing hook squirms
into your clever opposable thumb)

There's a halo of insects between us & nature

Where you pace has no walls & no corners (how
do you stop)   The thickets & mud flats are watching
Shall we pack up & leave, or join in their tangles

Think of our forebears, building their walls
all over the forest, firing the trees
the beasts & the earth till they choked on fire,
wondering why God had set down flowers
here, in the interminable waste of the forest,
where none but wild animals could ever behold

Think of their counting, alone in the winters,
how many windows, how many acres
imposed on the land, how many cupfuls
of flour, of salt, how many times
this sorting & counting: the last defense
against nature

The Heavy One

backwoods settler, Ontario, 18—.

Those pilgrims that, in the midst of bodily peril, yet malinger in their hearts, cherishing some irrecoverable, common loss, will find their burdens here the heavier grown.

—Advice to the Immigrant, 18—.

I cannot lift my limbs so high.

The trees here choke & stunt
another's growth: their limbs encircle,
scar; young birch against young pine they thrust
at heaven a savage basketry
of not quite deadly wounds, of which
the one, or both, must die.
                              Each wide wind
harvests them.
                    Their gloom below
entrammels me, makes numb my thoughts, disgusts
& overcomes all prior hope.
                              What use this continent?

I see my kindred, zealous to beat back
the interminable gollm which shadows me about,
enflame their land: in the furnace of their hope
I breathe defeat.
                    I cannot bear
their speech, their teeth like brittle stones,
exposed.
              I would not them infect.

In the shanty's doorhole light, the young ones
tumble like young animals in spring; my wife
then pulls a smile, & turns to me,
as though she found some warmth.
                              But I have seen
their faces rise in darkness, mingled, rolling,
their thin hands grope like roots
upon the boulders of their skulls; they drown
upon this muddy flux we called America;

3

they cannot foot our greed; they struggle
& they drown.
                    I would not them infect.

I am a low place, overgrown, where gloom
takes root. Nor pride nor drink
no longer warm me as they warm the others
of my kind. They kicked me back to life, that night
I fit my bulging Adam's fruit
into my knife's clean collaring; they thought
me drunk, & cured me as they cured themselves,
with curses & stale mockery. Warmed by their hate
I lived, through that cruel rescuing;
my red blood caked, my lungs heaved hold
& snared me here.
                    Above my ken
the forest canopy grows light, grows bright;
the ignorant leaves break forth
& frolic in that sun I cannot
reach.
            Does God take pity on the furtive lives
that huddle here in gloom, the timid
snouts that seek the dark?
                    Or does He
from His canopy of light throw down
on those who would not Him offend, but cannot
praise, His blazed reproach?

Concerning Survival

Where the wild escarpment breaks off into air,
where the caprock offers no footing for soil,
I see how the stunted oak survives:
older than I am, probably, waist-high,
scoured & lopped by the wind, it lives;
half of it dead, the other fool half
growing again while it can, between winters.

& I think of all the rigorous American
myths: of the trust we place in toughness,
of the honor we give to grim endurance,
& the faith we have that struggle is real;
& I think of the scorn we cast on the fattened
timber of valleys, & the deep mistrust
we feel for the easy machines we use.

& I remember the despair of the real pioneers
facing survival; & their ready complaints
about stones & darkness & useless wild things;
& their longing for softness, while they starved & bloated,
dreaming of meadows, of the easy hedges
& safe mild blossoms of home.

& I consider now the succeeding species
of wealth: the cars we command, the all-weather
conveyor-belt roads, the nationally advertised
gear for the wilderness parks. & I look
to the edge where the wild escarpment breaks
its starveling trees, where the oak stands braced
for another winter, rooted in stone:

the edge where the myths of my people survive.

The Artifact

He lived on a V of avalanched stone
shed from the cliff, scarcely greened over,
the only levels that the forest left open.
His cabin door framed the enormous white cliff
that was still falling down, a river of stone
aiming for him, & no hump of land
or fence to deflect it. He was never safe
but he didn't get buried when the treed land did.
When he sang from his stoop, or howled at the snow,
his voice went up to a smudge in the cliff,
a dead-black socket, a chimney of emptiness
that swallowed his syllables whole. When he peed
in the drifts his water froze like cheap
yellow beads, like an animal's markings, like his eyes
going tawny from drink. He trapped alone
with no voice but his own to remind him which
was the creature with paws in the trap & which
wasn't trapped, was him, was his own furry paws
working the traps. While the tallow lasted
he could eat almost anything & not throw it up.
He made good money, he used old lists
to remind him what people did with their money.
Fur money, snow money, money for living
alone like a coot, year after year,
surrounded, until he forgot what it was
to be among people, their quirks & the smell
of their cunning pink hands.

Now his cabin lies rotting in the V of stone
he inhabited. There's a trail for the summer hikers,
& the forest has Indians, hired by the day
to dig rocks from the trail, make the wilderness smooth.
His rafters & roof are gone into mold,
the precious nails stolen. The hikers picnic
on what's left of his logs, eating fresh peaches,
comparing their gear, vaguely aware
that it must have been hard to belong to this place.
From the cabin's doorhole a pink-legged sportsman
measures the cliff, remarks that artifacts
(this cabin, the inhabited site) breed flies.

6

The Friend

You are going into the wilderness, O.K., O.K.
Do you mind if I check, have you matches enough,
the heavens might drip? What about mirrors,
do you know how to signal, & suppose the compass
goes out of whack? Have you buttoned your pockets?
You're not a natural-born cave man, you know.
Will you carry I.D.? My book says your maps
can't be relied on. Supposing it snows,
you've heard of crevasses? If you intend to write
(or even to think), where will you sit?
If something comes hunting for you, will you kill it?
You can always eat tree bark, you can always call home
& I'll pay. But what shall I do with your turtle,
in case it escapes? What about mail?
Are you sure you're carrying your own address,
& your three kinds of notebooks to write on—
the used-up, the partly used, & also the new?
I worry about you, uprooted, surrounded
by green things with roots that don't talk
& stone things with no roots, not talking at all.
Are you trying to survive (you know you won't like it,
all by yourself), & how can I get you, out there?

Loving a Mountain

for Red Eagle

I

Loving a mountain is not
easy. You will have to take it, stone
by stone, into your hands & your skin
& into the space in your head that is prepared
for mountains. You will need a very large
emptiness, a very large need
in yourself: you will have to be willing to move
impediments (your habits of eating, of reason) out.
To encompass a mountain requires
"a twat like a horse-collar," an enormous
appetite; the hole in your head will have to be
made larger, by you. (You cannot expect the mountain
to help.) The winds will conspire to trick you,
the lichens shift
under your feet. The trees will ignore you,
the birds throw stones. If you try to move fast, expect
to fall off. You will have to wait till you have become
(in a sense) that mountain.

Loving a mountain is not easy
(or mutual, or useful at all).

II

You will have to learn how to learn
the slopes & the steepness, the places that welcome
your intrusion, the ponderous folds & wrinkles
where trees clamber upwards. Learn where the mountain
is tired, where it's unwilling to hold any more,
underfoot or over your head. Learn
the days when the ledges are happy & the great folds smile,
basking like pigs in the light. Stop being jealous
of the dust & the fauna: they got here first
& besides have adapted
better than you will: of course the mountain prefers
them. Learn when it wants you
to get off its back: stop staring, stop grabbing,
stop thinking of it.

III

The mountain is there, a mountain. It is not
inside you. It has all it can do
being a mountain. It does not want
to be loved.
             Or, your patience has not been sufficient:
maybe only a glacier could move slowly enough,
carry enough weight, to come to grips
with a mountain. Or maybe the problem is you,
who can't settle for being part of a mountain
in the way that the ignorant tree roots, the insects & pebbles,
are part.
             Your expensive techniques of survival,
your comforts, your ideas have cost you
this mountain: go back
where you came from.
                    Raise parsley,
it's attainable.

             Or maybe
(oh day of all blessings) in the back of your head the mountain
will move
lumpishly, creaking like the masts of a distempered ship,
suddenly, ponderously becoming
your mountain.

Nature is not like you & me, dear,
whatever its virtues it doesn't have hands
& it isn't our garden   If the inhabitants
squeak to each other, if the stones understand
what hooks them to earth, that does us no good
The clever things hide when they hear us, & the rest
move so godawful slow, we can't notice, or follow
A strange kind of time is elapsing, outside
of our watches   We can't make the mountains conform
to the lines on our maps   They slide in the night
& when we're not looking   Between boulder & boulder,
forest & scree, summit & summit,
there aren't any numbers   There is only the earth

We are surrounded
                    by boulders, by mountains
by passes as high up & as cold as mountains
This so-called valley was shed from a mountain
& that sky going black up over the summits
has eaten the last of our flares (no answer)

There's a perfect night view of the mountains behind us,
a real panorama, just like the brochures,
but it's bigger & colder & harder than us
Let's talk about something more human: my hands
in your pockets, you're ticklish, & who left the grease
in the stewpot again, & why is the bedrock
on my side of the tent   My watch says it's 8
& here comes the moon with her merciless light
so where is the flash

No matter how far in we go, how long
we are what we are
                    unnatural, human

In the Cave

for Cassandra

Here, in the mountains where stones prevail
where the trees squeeze upwards between boulders that move
& the water has no place to go but down
we have camped in a gap in the cliff, leaving
no messages   We think we are going to survive
here, in the winter that's coming

You, the adult
are busy building a defensible cave
All day I hear your stones falling, dislodged
to fill up old gaps, or open new ones,
to deflect (it is autumn) the coming downfalls
of snow & more stone

I (the other adult)
inspect my animals, all of them dead
dismembered & freezing, stores for the winter
I have also stockpiled descriptions of roots,
& maps for further escapes, & chants
in praise of the winter's radiant snows
(which have yet to descend)

Meanwhile the child we ignore
works in a dark burrow, part of the cave
we can't enter   She says there are monsters in there
who speak with feathers & tongues   We don't listen
She is busy defacing the walls of her cavern
with spittle & blood
                    (only her work
will be found)

What are you doing, trying to paw
 your way uphill over raw logging cuts,
scrabbling up stream beds, breaking through thickets,
 as though it mattered which way you went?
 Those are hands not paws growing out of your arms

Red-faced & huffing, strapped to your shadow like a coolie
strapped to your ripstop weatherproof pack
strapped to romantic notions of nature—
which by the way occurred in fields
& meadows, i.e., in civilized lands
you enormous kid, running loose on a tether
Your body connects to a car in a lot, below

The hawks don't want you out here, they're too ignorant
to beg for your garbage   The bears & the clever
mammals avoid you   The trees are just trees,
they all look alike   The stones have no numbers
no shapes you remember (but they seem to multiply)
Did you come all this way to gibber with stones?

You don't belong here (did you ever, & where)

What are you proving, importing yourself
& your gear to the wilds?   Your daily calories
exceed the environment   What you can gather
is sour, or breaks, & besides you are queasy
about killing
                    You stop on a ridge & the safe water gurgles
out of your plastic container into your mouth
In your left breast pocket the keys to the car
are jingling
                    You can always go back
You always go back

In the Midst of Winter

In snowy ravines, when I should be relishing
the steady downhissing of flakes from the sky
& the white soft drift from the tree tufts, I imagine
hot baths
in a claw-footed tub, steaming & deep
in a heavy barrel, up to my shoulders
like Queen Guinevere (oh to be her
& not my forebears hauling the buckets)
hot springs
odorless, crystalline, deep & secluded
hot shelves
in a sauna, almost too hot to keep breathing

In the midst of wild winter
I want to be pink as a blister all over
& freed
of these sweated trail clothes, these heavily stiffening
thighs, these toes going cold when I halt,
these fears that keep me checking the sky,
the shadows, the trail, my strength & my chocolate,
as I haul my weight on through the wintry forest

Later, in the armchair where I plod through white pages,
through the harmless dry rustle, through the wintry tracks
of the print & my straggling scribble, I imagine
white blizzards
margins of error in a whitening tundra,
the packs abandoned, the body still trudging,
its tissues cannibal, its vision snowblind
white flakes downhissing
on the wild dark mere where Beowulf surfaces,
bloodied & cold, a monster at elbow
white glaciers surging,
virgin as laundry, beneath the glittering
swoop of my plane & the flight of my skis

Beyond this winter,
beyond the warmth-seekers, I'll race with the Snow Queen
free
from this furnace that keeps me secure, this roof
that shuts out the sky, these windows sealed
against sneezes, these plowable neighborhood snows
that sugar the lawns & plump the white porches

As I doze I remember
white drifts
Over my sock feet they gather, beautiful,
lustrous, hissing soft welcomes

The Observers

The glacier disappoints you:
it resembles (you observe,
through binoculars) not snow
but rather, soiled underwear.

How right you are,
I agree.
       Strange,
how your underwear, discarded
(I later observe)
does not resemble
a glacier at all.

You don't like the glaciers we see, they're messy
retreaters; you have tastes & real standards, you prefer
the less obtainable advancers, the clean
blue destruction you expected from glaciers

Unfortunately all of the locals are shrinking,
getting dirtier each year, their snouts melt off
& the rubble exposed isn't pretty; it's rock
& grey muck & grey dust, even the tarns
& the rapids that come from these glaciers are dirty

Well we could always come back in a couple millenia
when Xmas card spruces have covered the dirt
& the *gletschermilch* has been flushed from the waters

or wait for another Ice Age
to unify shapes, clean up the scene

Why can't you take Nature as offered?
Shut up & be grateful, you can't afford
your private dynamite, so don't interrupt

Out on the ice it's our one chance to listen
to whatever the glacier is muttering, to see
how this great swollen hunk & its Neanderthal drains
are ploughing the bedrock   Here we can notice
how accidentally the glacier creates
soil & water, valley & life

Look, we are mammals, tramping the surface
The warmth we have
                              is small & not lasting

Process, with Questions

Like a glacier I keep dumping
great mounds of moraine between us:
loose stones, loose hairs, souvenirs

I know my winter advances
are slow but they do (with the help
of your occasional thaws) accumulate

Is it a bridge or a blockade I'm building?
you ask (your voice echoing
& echoing, a long ways above me)

Which do you want? I evade
Should I fill up the distances (impassable
except for goat hoofs) you claim

Or would you rather admire
the girth of the boulders between us
which prove I'm retreating from you?

Boundary Waters

If a dream recurs, is it real?

I know where I am, on the edge of which portage,
but why am I waiting, woods hat in hand,
on this leech-ridden rock?
                                        Is it for these voyageurs
coming out of the forest, these sportsmen whose faces
gleam hollow under the hulls of canoes
they carry upturned like great silver beaks?
Do I want them to signal, call me off this bedrock
& into that channel? Why am I eyeing
their muscular tans, their strides, their expensive
specialty boots? By hunger or greed
could I enter their shapes, if I watch them closely
& carry them into my eyes?
                                        The trees grow darker
after each launching, the clouds close in
There's a continent back there, blooming with darkness
I can't take it in, or survive in these wilds
(no knife, no matches, only a map
I tied to a stone & threw to the waters)

& now the gap in the forest disgorges
particular humans (some grownups whose names
I have used, a child I have cause to remember)
They're loading the familiar gear   Their faces
turn to each other as they paddle away,
singing a Methodist hymn I remember
They are happy together
                                        Light breaks from the clouds
as the humans dwindle, mirages   Light flows
like a pathway of cold over the waters
The dream I have lived spills open   I am left
life-sized & breathing, crossing the bedrock

When you are free, where doesn't matter

18

The Dream

In this dream (which is happy)
the canoe I am in lurches (no reason) mid-channel
overturns in a deep dark water   The shore
is so far I don't see it   My gear spills out
like lopsided blossoms, floating & floundering
down to the bottom   I watch it all sink
my notebooks unfinished   3 years irrecoverable
poems visions trivia no one else saw
will see or remember

Now in this dream I am diving (how bravely)
straight down like a loon   I pierce through the water
so swiftly, my feet have somehow grown webs
But the notebooks have opened, the wet pages flutter
away in the darkness, petals or suckers dispersing
I cannot save many, choosing, abandoning
the past to the past

Scrabbling out of the depths (somehow, just barely)
I surface, my 2 hands clutching all the blank pages
dripping, which prove (this is the happiness)
there are poems that will be

Leaving the Wilderness Campsite
Boundary Waters

I

A rectangle of dryness, bent seedlings, roots
cramped by our tent. A few hairs
on tree bark, imprints of shoes
(partial, blurring) near the waterline.
Under rotted red larch, human
manure. The surrounding lake made smaller
by several potfuls of water.
Dead branches subtracted, burnt for our comfort
to charwood & ash. & (earlier) a flaring of heat,
a trailing of smoke on the nearest trees.

Such traces we leave.

II

What are *they* saying, the rightful inhabitants
of thicket & pathway, fur & wing,
about us? What thinking, what smelling,
now we are gone?
                    Are they grateful
for their own kind of silence reopened,
their own kind of gathering & fear?

Or, are they creatures already corrupted,
simple scavengers lured to prefer
more middens to rummage, more of the easy
garbage to gorge on, more of the glittering
shards & the jagged queer-smelling metals
left by the dominant sportsmen before us?

What do *they* make, of us & our leavings?
& how could we know?—we who translate
flickerings into our words, creatures
into our species, the unanswering wilderness
into our myths (as in this poem's
hypotheses)—
                    in the wilds *they* inhabit
what remembers our questions, our traces?

III

Bright ripples, bright metal, the flanks of the canoe
lift from the land shade riding the shallows,
swing out into open lake, our ripples
blur & slide over.   Suddenly behind us,
the forest heals shut—
                              no glimmerings left,
no watchers, no trace.

The Trees in the Peaceable Meadow

A steady rumble   of water sliding
sideways & down   in gorges below
Trickles of water   swelling the limestone
sediments floating   shales giving way
The water's tendrils   probing at bedrock

What has that got to do with us,
ask the trees   in the peaceable meadow
over the gorge
                    We have grown accustomed
to the rumble of water   adjacent, below us
to the plenteous soil   in the craw of our roots
to the unmoving strata   of stone below us
stone going down   to a center of stone

We have never feared water
                              We have heard of changes
dissatisfied waters   in other valleys
probing, uprooting   original faults
of spruce undercut   & high firs wrenched
from their sockets   into a suddenly opening depth

But how many channels   are actually cut,
out of all the meadows   there be?

&, if this rumbling & scrabbling of water
did concern us,   well, what could we do,
till it happened?
                    (Besides, even if trouble is coming
under our strata,   it may not come
in our time)
                    say the trees in the peaceable meadow

who are founded more surely   than any creature
upon the plates   of the floating earth

Under the Red Pines

Under the red pines   fir seedlings are blades
pointing up through the snow   Are wedges aiming
for sky   Are scantlings   drooping & fragile
& yet symmetrical   their trunks as spindly
as the arm bones of children   Are stragglers leaning
on heavy snow
                    This is a war
over land, over species   over every snowflake
& drizzle   A war already won

Under the red pines   the hemlocks cluster
as if for shelter   their symmetrical branches
thriving in shade   Over them tower
the monstrous red trunks   of the ancestor pines
At the top of the forest   the dominant tufts
wag in the sunlight   like the crests of warriors
triumphant   League upon league of red trunks
their wizened grey arms   broken in shade

Under the red pines   fir seedlings are spears
thrusting up   Are wedges opening the sky

The Fault

In the metal mirror I hold to the wilderness
I see: a wilderness cornered & level,
revealed as if through a window's lense

My eye traverses strata of cliffs,
lake in the center, linear streams,
these dark isosceles trees going up

But staring too close to the image, I see
how a fault in the mirror crooks the straight trees
into bubbly sky   Like a subsurface rock

it breaks the surface mirror of lake
Where the white creeks fall, logically, downwards,
the fault in the mirror dislodges their falling,

upheaves the great established faults
which raised these strata, which hold this lake
like a mirror held in the palm of a hand

& now I see clearly where the high peaks leap
in a whorling, great stones thrown back to dust
as in the unwitnessed whorls which shaped this earth

My eye traversing this loosened image
falters, is confused, the pupil widens,
blurs & expands, its particles swimming

(how readily) back, into the chaos
that was & will be

The Table

It was a place where board-lengths do not exist,
where corners & walls do not exist,
a place where all angles gape stupidly open
Wave piles upon wave, slippery, shifting,
too quick for the eye   The sand grains twist
their uncountable facets, the better to dazzle you
At the edge of the dunes, driftwood & live wood
entangle, warping & blooming & rasping,
while their buried members subside in the sand

Alone in this wilderness, I found a table,
full-scale, intact (having ridden what storms?),
washed up & laid on its side   Its squared
oak planks stood up like a target, rebutting
the amorphous winds   Its right-angled legs
held straight in the sand   In all that waste
it was the only made thing   I admired it, & knelt
to haul it upright on its own 4 legs,
like a table   I wanted the years to respect it,
the beetles & weeds to take shelter beneath
It could say to the wilderness *Here is something not yours,*
 something still here & not broken

But when I tried to lift it, by the bottommost edge,
the slanted oak planks shot apart in my hands,
dropped down, guillotines all, on my shins
I couldn't gather a surface together
So I left it there, its framework empty
& braces exposed, its planks splayed out
all ways, like slats on a ruined coop
The small waves chuckled beside me, & the dune weeds
sighed at my back
                    Aristotle was right
(& my shins are learning): a thing is its usage:
& a table that is through with being a table
is not a table at all

In the Absence of Humans

for Margaret Atwood

In the absence of humans, things change,
slowly   A kind of growth,
a readying for growth, sets in
The stones of the fire circle,
three days behind us, abandoned,
drift heavily open   New bracken
invades our footholds   The land
rebounds   Where our bodies were
the waters heal over, no traces

      Meanwhile, in the city we left
      nature keeps trying, somehow
      Rain flushes the air, industrial
      soot settles sideways & down
      along with the pigeons, used papers,
      used leaves, coughs & debris
      & the rest of the cosmic mantle
      The paved earth thickens, getting ready
      for roots, for rain & decay

Where the granite began, two hours
behind us, the snake slides back
& sleeps on the trail   In the lense
of your compass, lost among boulders,
moisture like root hairs gathers
Over our tracks the spiderwebs
close   The air closes over
Your scream & the sound of your falling
belong to the leaves, no echo

In the rooms we left, new strata
silt over the untended levels
Our implements clog, my notebooks
revert to gibberish   Memories
break loose from the artifacts   Our fingerprints
drift   Crevices widen,
the foundation shifts & trickles
towards old burrows   In the earth,
in the air, spores swell, pouring in

Noon, & we halt on some beach,
not clear on the map   Three ridges
of boulders, still moving, no cedar
Around us the land rebounds
from the last glacial age   Skinned bears,
we swim among stones   Words float
out of my head, my mouth
garbles your name, I'm losing
my fear   We begin to belong

Untitled Love Poem

What is this precious
space between us
we protect with our warmth?
Why are we circling

& keeping it empty,
struggling to enter,
or cross it, get through it,
but always re-entering?

Our muscles don't answer
(they are older than questions)
they bend & they follow
the pull of something like tides

something that causes
the hollows in water
& mud flats that creates
the seeds & the animal chambers

something that covers
what we see in darkness,
in the hooded sockets of eyes,
in the caverns of dreams

something that makes everywhere
in valleys, in fossils,
the shape of the warm
primordial shelter

Another Untitled Love Poem

What mammal are you, what whale
                          blowing & rising
what creature or drifter
                          washed up on what shore
In the darkness of bodies you
                          are the hollows & slopes
the ridges of land
                          & the-slippery seas
the heavy invisible planet
                          pulling my senses
The fleece of your belly & legs
                          is tangled, alive
an undergrowth rippling
                          on a strange warm earth
In this harboring darkness we jostle
                          like swimmers or craft
swung round in what waters
                          like waters moving
against & into each other
                          Your body
is a place unfathomed
                          a headland emerging
from darkness
                          My muscles are barriers
                          are channels
sliding toward you
                          pulsing & sliding
Wait, the boundaries are changing
                          The skins
which held us
                          separate/give way
                          We float
two creatures sensed
                          in a ponderous darkness
whose darkness or place
                          I have always/
will never remember

You emerge into sleep
                    I watch, drifting off
Your body is yours
                  a vessel on course
an open, familiar shore
                    I need not discover

November

The flat cold sky, no distance in it,
no orange, no warmth.   Small grey birds
left behind in the alleys, picking at litter.
Cracks in the asphalt, grey sockets
drawing apart like a wound.   The soft
insufficient brick walls, the yellowish windows
of inhabited buildings.   Overhead
a last flock crosses the dour grey air,
their black wings flutter like ashes, so high,
have they escaped.   The elm trees stiffening
& rasping, branch against branch, abandoned.
Leaves starved for sap, sloughed off, a flaccid
deterioration underfoot,
even the bright leaf colors are rotting,
leaching down in the hardened soil.
                                        November.
When life's not wanted. The grim menstruation
of the earth.   Part of a cycle,
oh sure, & the ice age is over & done with,
but meantime this stingy debris turning colder,
a bad time for mammals, when will it end.

In Praise of the Natural Flowing

Out of the storm pipe, between the old path
& the unsold lots, the water journeys
at will this winter, flowing & floating
over its sheathing of ice: I see the clear riffles
angling & falling seaward; the continents
forming & formed, where ice, mud,
weedstuff & human discards run aground;
the channels & shallows forced between continents;
the reed clumps hummocked & footed like trees
with silt & debris; & down through the water
a fragile mud-tissue holding, half-shielding
the dead mingled leaves & the fragments of weeds,
like wingstuff in amber; the reed stalks prone,
combed out like the hairs of a long-drowned beast;
& the powdery silt & the clear openings in silt
where the water has winnowed its earth: I see
beside the water the gradual shelvings
of ice, contoured like land, reaching out
from its shorings & ending; & over the still places
the frail film ice, transparent as cirrus
or the membranes which form over the unborn:

I see in this world the natural flowing,
older than Genesis, slower than clouds
but faster than stone, which forms the rivers,
the lowlands & channels & continents of earth:
which feeds on life & tends ever towards life:

& I praise it, in gratitude & bitterness, knowing
this flow, vulnerable & beautiful, is permitted
to be this winter, between the worn path
& the scrawny stakes with the flapping red plastic
which claim this world.

Human Love Poem

Sun wakes us, & the squirrels yell
from ice-slick limbs.   You grope my breast,
I curl around your helpless warmth
& give you suck.   Small skull, small foot,
I am the river of your thirst:
the first of caves your hunger fills:
the blood in your warm fontanel:
the sheltered slope you burrow in:
the murmur & the breath & the pulse
we drift into your feeding sleep.

Outside, beyond your pulsing head,
tree shadows vein our neighbors' ice-
slick roofs.   The ice-starved animals
break elder buds, avoid the human
bread we put beneath the tree;
their young go hungry, cold, go nowhere
in our subdivided world.
Is it the fit survive?   My species'
cunning & its luxuries
prevail: therefore in helpless warmth

you nuzzle, suckling, predator
as I am predator, the fierce
inheritors of earth: therefore
I do what any creature would:
I turn to you, & feed my young.

On the Other Side of the Wall

As I write about nature, not knowing,
in the attic the insistent starling

scrabbles uphill & uphill & drops,
trying to get out to the cheeps

of its young on the eaves boards, but the hill
is all wall, scrabbles up to the hole

in the wall, but the hole is all screen,
scrabbles uphill & flops & again,

& I think it is squirrels on the roof,
or my neighbor, making improvements,

or my son in his crib, half-waking,
as the starling flops uphill & breaks

something inside, so it stops
where I find it, limp on the steps

to the attic, black feathers, no struggle,
but it seems to take in a little

of the water I hurriedly spill
by its beak, but it lies there, too still,

as I take it, gently, outside
with water, & crumbs in a diaper,

it lies there, black hoods on its eyes,
& will not wake up or climb back

to the shelter/the trap where it died.

Equivalencies

The fear of not writing, of having no words:

is the muscles not working, the pack topheavy,
the hard slime on ledges where the ankle gives way:

is the sledge-hammer current at the bottom of waves
coming too fast & the swimmer unable:

is the baby hung up in the birth canal,
the contractions building but its heartbeat stalls:

is the hemorrhage of vision with nothing made yours:
is the flicker of brain waves in the same stuck dream.

The writing is easy, the having is easy:

is the meadows opening, is the blessing of speed
in the mouth of the runner, is the long easy strides

riding & passing the crests of the earth,
is the surge of delivery, is the new being riding

the pulsing red channel, is the mountains riding
the slower upheavals of strata & drift,

is the white surge riding the hull of the seed
as it breaks into life, is the spillover couplet

& the words coming through, is the deep dream opening
& the words coming true, the words
                              coming through

The Man

See, a small space in the woods,
green overgrown with green,
shadows trees brush entangled
At the edge of the clearing a man
a white man, middle-aged, aging
just his face stands out in the dimness
"dominion over every living thing"
a hunters' jacket, hunters' cap
He lifts the spear of his rifle barrel
aims
with cold, hard, arthritic hands
16 years on the line, finally made foreman,
finally inspector, finally retired
The cold, square, aging jaws of the man
are barely flushed, a tingle of fear
or pleasure as he aims

diagonally across the clearing
into the black furry mass of the bear
She sits on her haunches, back to a stump,
an ancient, massive, dog-nosed brute
pawing the dogs
who yap & skitter away
(My mother's mother, huge in her dress,
sits in the creek, swatting the water & laughing)
She is warm, stupid; she smells of bear
an abundance of flesh, stumpy limbs,
stone of a head & little pig eyes
teats where she rears, in the black close fur
She smells like my mother/my mother's mother
she does not understand
she won't get away

The man with the rifle aiming
confers with the other shadowy men
ranging the edge of the clearing
Each in position: they have agreed
which one will have her/whose turn it is
One of them covers the kill

My mother does not understand
rears, paws, shakes her head & its wattles of fur
thinking she's won

Afterwards the body is hoisted
"a sack full of lard" on inaccurate scales
is hung, dressed, weighed on accurate scales
The skull (unshattered, unhurt) is found eligible
for Boone & Crockett official measuring
The head is stuffed & mounted

                              safe on the walls
where every evening he enters, approaches
fires recoils fires into the small stupid eyes
"the thrill of a lifetime" my mother

The Dominant Species

At the edge of the freeway lanes,
where the concrete slabs thin out
into shoulders, & the graded embankments
override the earth, erosion

takes root   The crevices widen,
go deep like a plant, & feed
on salt, winter ice, pressure
of traffic, thaw & more ice

Slowly, interminably, the concrete
gives way   Its littered edges
revert to rubble & air,
to a precarious scum of soil

where tumbleweeds (native to salt flats,
to deserts—how did they get here?)
hole up, sprout & blossom,
survive somehow, through these winters

At the edge of your windshield you see them,
at 60 or 70, green tangles
in cracks, surrounded but growing,
bouncing back in the gusts from the traffic

It's comforting to know
that Nature's still there after all
These stunted barbed-wire plants
are prying the concrete & winning

too slowly   By the time you exit,
40 on the ramp, slowing down,
in the fields behind you new freeways
have opened   In the lots around you

the concrete is spreading, faster
& further than anything live
Nature's ignorant, can't compete
with our species, can't adapt at our speeds

A Clean, Well-lighted Place

Open the door & step in: everything here
is better than average but not really beautiful:
the sauce on the ribs (or whatever you order)
will be thicker than usual but not unique;
the view & the lighting will be skillfully blended,
blue & blue-green with glitters above;
& the wood & wood-grain, a little bit better
than last year's model

& as for us, the inhabitants,
we are all white & healthy all over
(even the bus boys have blue eyes & tans)
& every table is headed by father
husband or brother or bachelor man
No one is missing a limb or his senses
no one's incontinent or grievously lonely
or poor or otherwise different

No one, certainly not ourselves
who have worked all our lives to deserve
this haven

Time Frame/Shiawassee Ravine/Going Back

In the Silurian saucer, cold water, packed leaves,
cold mud.   The white glare of winter drained off.
Thin weeds on the flanks of the great ravine,
our boots going down, new runnels.   No creatures,
no tracks.   Only the creek is alive,
muddy, opaque, spate from the woods'
surviving acres. We head upstream.
Gouged valley of ice, a mile overhead
sheeting this spot, before & after
these humans, this warmth.
                              Now the hung clouds hover,
bellies of rain or of snow.   Now the black
once-dominant elms sport blackbird & crow,
flash of a redwing.   Now locust & hawthorn,
bush-size, clogging the 4-wheel ruts
of the hunters we follow.   Are we innocent?   Upstream
the grey second growth of the woods, grey blur
on the ancient ridges, strata & thrust,
what do we know?
                              On the far ridge (don't look)
the colonials rise, glass & white siding,
asking 50 to 80, clear-cut, a climax
of species, of peoples, what's ecology, & who
can afford the wild?
                              Trespassers, no answers,
we follow old paths, scanning the tracks
of glacier & melt, gathering the cold
grey flickering evidence of spring, remembering
in tangle & weed-tree, cloud-spawn & mud,
the stubborn forebears of all our life.

Dream/Poem

The water's receding
                          We stand on the picturesque sands
a life boat apart
                          (but there aren't any boats)
As usual, we cannot agree
                              what danger exists
if I saw it first
                   You are taking pictures
of curious formations
                          exposed on the sea floor
The space between waves gets bigger
                                     You tell me that's safety
I've read *Reader's Digest*
                         I know who'll survive

The child grabs my hand
                            & we run for the cliff
(I called to you both)
                         through mud & old shale
We have to get higher
                      the far tufts above
Scrabbling in clay
                   almost stepped on her hand
I have to keep going
                      my hostage to fortune
These mucky ravines
                      between us & safety
worse than the sands
                      We'll be scoured away
These bushes are useless
                      I tell her to use them

The wave could be slowed
                            on the long sloping bottom
The wave could be fed
                      on the bodies of tourists

who are swimming below us
                        splashes & echoes
a whale of an outing
                        They agree on what's real
Fathers with cameras
                        shoot from their car tops
the chance of a lifetime
                        Your angle is better
You swam on the team
                        Stick figure in surf
posing or shooting
                        Have you got one of us

We go over the top
                        & the earth looks different
lawns & flat paths
                        All settled, no danger
A white frame house
                        with square pillared porches
Old people, old women
                        They have lived here forever
I remember the woodlot beyond
                        (Tree roots too shallow
not properly thinned
                        Wood is no shelter)
I look back to the edge
                        All peaceful, no swimmers
just light in the air
                        from the risen waters
(The reel of the dream
                        skips backwards: did you follow or not
slipping below us
                        when I couldn't turn back?)

Now I walk among strangers
                    the child at my side
regarding the waters
                    blue-green & opaque
through a white picket fence
                         at the edge of the cliff
My parasol twirls
                    pink coin on the waters
In an earlier century
                    Father determined
our course on this earth
                         There was no turning back

Self-portrait

In search of a structure, a phrase
that will shake into being a structure,
the artist (myself) sits endlessly
staring out a vacant night window or into
the vacant reflection of a person slumped
over a mess of paper on a straight brown table
One hand of the person reaches for darkness
but stops at the window   Its fingers are empty
The head is a lean peasant head, no genius,
just hunger   The head avoids being seen
But the sideways eye is full of reflections,
of brightness & darkness, disordered, opaque
The other hand droops over the open mouth
which waits like an idiot
                              flower or trap
for words to fall into

Packing in with a Man

I had thought I would need him
                        love under stars
my fellow explorer
                        Packing into the badlands
following the earth
                        my needs were quite different

Where the hollows of foothills
                        opened their silence
he kept asking questions
                        Where the shoulders of cliffs
trusted our shadows
                        he plotted with maps
Wherever we went
                        he needed escapes
to the road & the car
                        to the money he trusted
When the nighthawk attacked
                        he timed its return
When the bright quartz signalled
                        he broke it for samples
When the fire worm began
                        he drowned it with napalm
In the high arroyos
                        his bootprints trampled
the fingers of cedar
                        the prints of the bones

He refused to follow
                        cloud furrows, brain furrows,
the buried windings
                        of water & silt,
the dirt track remembered
                        in a dream of creatures
I couldn't believe
                        enough for us both
So I took what I needed
                        Less shelter, more fear

Journey to the Interior

The way should be difficult, the terrain obscure
when you first set out. Perhaps it is better
to go it alone, mapless, trusting
to hunger & luck. Let the moon be empty
over your shoulder, the sky uncertain;
avoid the places where humans intrude,
the high wires, the roads; shake off their echoes:
at the rim of your eyes let nothing enter
that would not approve your going this way.

Look for the track of the lizard on bedrock,
for the narrower ledges & the stone-choked gorge;
where the stunted fir bends like a signal
follow its shadow. Look for the hollows
glittering below you, mica or water,
not to be trusted; better the tongues of dew
where the spiders drink, or your own face sweat.
When you rest remember that even the gnats
swarming mid-focus inhabit the dazzling
meandering strata you can only behold.
At the height of the sun it will become unclear,
between scrabbling downhill over open rock
& the forced ascents into the undergrowth,
whether you are climbing or falling, laboriously,
a stone in each hand & a stone for each foot,
back to the endless pits of the bush.
Keep going: a track, any track, smoothness
of dirt, a small fallen cairn, inexplicable
breaks in the bramble will tell you that something,
boulder or creature, has travelled this way,
though not in this year.

When you have come far enough
to be forced back in your reckoning, to perceive at last
that the slow scrabbles upwards & north have led you
apparently down in meandering directions,
then cast off your compass & offer your knife
silently to whatever has brought you thus far,
be it pull of the earth or a slanting of trees.
Keep going but go without thinking, step
without looking, trust the stones & the brambles to rise
in footholds under your weight. Remember
that others have come here, though not in your lifetime;
others, though not of your species, have feared
& believed & kept going, though not without losses
& error. Still the largest of trees you behold
must have entered their eyes; still the same stubborn granit
must have witnessed their struggle without revealing
its scars embedded, white among white,
that would blaze your way clear.

                        As it is you will blunder
in the marginal light, without warning or hope,
against the suddenly opening tangle
that rims the clearing into which you will stumble,
the place where the cedar mingle in welcome,
where the withheld light of the forest pours down
in a river of shining upon any creature,
rooted or stone. Heaved here at last,
beyond distance or lense, you will know the light enter
into the transient stone of your skull,
blazing your sight with its power, blazing
the tinder within you that belongs to this place,
blazing & blessing till you praise at last
the unbearable shining you have witnessed forever
in a place beyond memory or praise.

Untitled Stone Poem

I

There are places where the earth's cliffs stumble & break,
where the boulders have gathered & the sea waves abide,
places where stone clambers on stone,
skull-shape & slab, tumbling & mauling

There the animals retreat & go inland for water
There the humans retreat, no harbor, no paths
The grasses retreat, unable to seed
in the moving grey stones   There cedar roots grope,
feeding on stone, cramped & retreating

What light inhabits these barrens of stone
older than humans, borne across waters
no human beholds   What silence inhabits
these slow-heaving stones, & under that silence
what murmuring, learned from the ridges of water
falling into the land, mounting & falling

II

If you had the patience of God you could wait
for the fossils hidden in stone to awaken
for the scoured hollows of boulders to rise
for the fractures veining the granite to open
as thistle & flower, creeper & wing

Or, with the lesser patience of death you could wait
for the breath to subside & the flesh settle back
in the thickening mantle, mould among mould,
unspecified shards where the soft bones broke

Or, while the light on the water wavers
& the grey gelid sea drifts toward winter,
if you wait without speaking, without hours or maps,
the stones will begin to forget you are there
The cedars will rouse & turn to each other,
frond among frond, gravely embracing

& the light on the water will gather in fullness,
long barrows of light sliding into your eyes
as the sea slides into the stones & garners
slimecell & bubble, bright furrows of life

& the stones will speak, stone among stone
& stone among water, in a tongue that is known
to the skin of your eyes, a breath remembered
in the pit of your breath, a hymn of grey stone
that will enter the shining furrows of brain

& never translate into words for the humans

The Summer Woman

Sprawled on the mountain's flank, half-hidden
under apple leaves gone wild, she watched
the osprey hover above the cedars,
wheel & glide home.   Squinting she saw
the tinfoil gleam of the fish it had carried
from the glittering inlet, miles below.
Closing her eyes to the sun, she felt
the skulls of the nestlings thicken, warm
as an infant's skull under her hand;
she felt her own skull lift in the sun,
the layers of calcium thin out in the steep
bright air.
              Over the osprey's nest
the fronds of the cedars roused themselves,
stirred & subsided; she waited to feel
her own skin stir, hairs drift, as the invisible
wind descended, riffling the meadow
& its fringes of bracken around her, lifting
the low apple leaves, carrying & loosing
the voices of the men she'd borne, husband
& sons, far echoes absorbed by the forest.
Alone with the mountain, she breathed the wind
& the chill it bore from the cedars' darkness;
saw beyond seeing the packed mould shift
in the path they were building, the felled trees twist
out of their lines, the unnameable beetles,
cells, root hairs, devouring their work.
She had done enough.
                      Sleeping or waking,
the brightness slid by. She felt in her head
the mountain moving its haunches towards winter,
the meadow lie cramped under the drifts
of approaching snow, the cedars stiffening
in a brittle air, the talons of ice
clawing their trail & giving it back
to the mountain.

50

           Enough.   The warm bracken leaned
its fronds towards her; the meadow retreated,
root by root, from the invading wilderness;
the cedars rejoiced, green among green.
About her the ponderous slope of the mountain
wheeled & fell in its silent arc
away from the sun, bearing her breath
with its burdens, carrying the trace of her warmth
headlong in space, a chip on the surface,
wheeling & falling.

The Habit of Fire

By the wilderness lake I settle my haunches
in a nest of stones, lean back on a deadfall
carcass of pine, the only shelter,
cold but not wet.   Behind me thickets
waiting for nightfall; no openings my size,
no one's been here.   The sun slides down
over the green-black cones of the mountains
rimming the lake; the sky flares up
like a mirror, pearl on the water, glaring
& greying.   Suddenly thinned air, like water,
wraithes of cold swimming towards me;
too late to wash up.   Grey firestones & kindling
readied before me, unlit; deadfall
enough for hours.

Black mountains, black sky;
stone shapes changing.   I see through a face net
my personal aura of insects close in,
signalled by warmth.   Things crackling & listening
behind me; the sky goes Whooee, Whooee,
no one I know.

Smell of horses
from somewhere, then gone; no horses out here,
anything that big is probably bear.
New prints today on the logging road,
in the place where I backtracked for water, bear crossing
over the prints of my Vibram soles,
full-grown.   While I yawn the road I will follow
leans downhill, gullies, lets go; stones topple;
thickets I broke are healing behind me.
I don't want to know how the blackness spreads
under my ribs.
If I died out here
it would be my doing, not theirs; I smell
of textiles & fire; even dead they'd avoid me.
I couldn't live here.

                    In the blackness a lapping
of water or muzzle; the air says something,
gibberish or warning, & quits when I move,
matches in hand, to strike open the fire
that stops me from seeing.

Last Image

After the wilderness
the mind's photos recede,
blur & drop out

as the sprawl of the Rockies
cuts to the mirror
of the speeding auto

dips & goes under
the blank empty shoals
of the fenced-in prairies

as I follow the dominant
signs of the freeway
back to my kind

Judith McCombs has published widely in little and feminist magazines in the United States and Canada; her poems appear in *POETRY, LOON, POETRY NORTHWEST, APHRA, MOVING OUT, WAVES, PRISM,* etc. Her first book, *SISTERS & OTHER SELVES,* Glass Bell Press, appeared in 1976. Five of the Hilda poems from *SISTERS* were featured in the Bantam anthology *WE BECOME NEW,* edited by Iverson and Ruby. She has also published parables in the *LITTLE MAGAZINE, WOMEN: A Journal of Liberation,* and *HAPPINESS HOLDING TANK;* and a number of articles in women's studies and in Canadian literary criticism.

In 1971, Judith McCombs co-founded *MOVING OUT,* the nation's oldest surviving feminist literary magazine; her work appears in its anthology, *MOVING TO ANTARCTICA,* edited by Kaminski, published by Dustbooks. She teaches wilderness literature, creative writing, et. al., at the Center for Creative Studies, College of Art and Design in Detroit. She is currently writing a series on Atwood, and another on how women nature writers conceive nature.

"The *AGAINST NATURE* poems come from the Bruce Trail, the Boundary Waters, and the Rocky Mountains, in the states and Canada. The old settler accounts of this terrain bear witness that our forebears distrusted 'the interminable wilderness' in which they were so desperately busy trapping, chopping, firing, and otherwise destroying. Even in 'isolation' and danger they clung all the more to the quaint human habits and projects they had imported, like china, numbers, fences, into the wilderness. I see modern backpackers, myself included, doing the same thing, with our guaranteed calories and water, our weatherproof zippers and shelters, and above all our fierce dependencies on map, compass, watch. It seems that the more we love the wilderness, and the further in we go, the more we have to act human, to keep apart from nature, lest it engulf us and stop our getting back, to our time and our kind. And yet we do pack in, temporarily, partially, bringing to nature our own (unnatural) wonderment and love."

photo by Ernst Benjamin